Dog Woman

For permissions and information on ordering books, contact
operations@smallharborpublishing.com.

Cover art: Jill Noll, "Untitled"
Cover design: Diana Baltag
Interior design: Eliza Carlson
Publisher: Allison Blevins
Executive Editor: Kristiane Weeks-Rogers
Managing Editor: Bianca Dagostino

DOG WOMAN
MELINDA FREUDENBERGER
ISBN 978-1-957248-69-1
Harbor Editions,
an imprint of Small Harbor Publishing
Special thanks to: The Wild & Precious Life Series and Kristin Vandeventer

Dog Woman

Melinda Freudenberger

Harbor Editions
Small Harbor Publishing

Contents

Dog Woman

To be a dog woman is not necessarily to be downtrodden; that has very little to do with it. In these pictures every woman's a dog woman, not downtrodden, but powerful. To be bestial is good. It's physical. Eating, snarling, all activities to do with sensation are positive. To picture a woman as a dog is utterly believable.

—Paula Rego

It's the end of days. BABY is standing naked in front of her home's bay window—blinds open, the lights in her living room emanating from behind her like she is God's son, like she is one bright headlight facing down a black road. Otherworldly—how her neighbors' homes bathe the grass with golden light, how the moon is so close it could kiss, how her blood leaks in a slick hot trail down the middle of her thigh.

How ready is BABY to speak plainly? It's been three hours since it happened. Consider that stretch of time both the length of a rope wrapped around the earth three times, and the length of a rope wrapped around BABY's neck once. Pull—don't look away.

Outside, the jagged edge of a branch split in two attempts to pierce through the night sky. The branch fell off a few weeks ago during a storm and took everything below out with it. BABY had eyed the city workers suspiciously as they cut more branches off and hauled them away in big trucks, leaving what looked like knives protruding from its trunk, lifted and glinting in the moonlight of their own accord.

Three texts, three seconds apart, three hours ago. The first: *condom broke*. The second: *wtf u said u weren't a virgin*. The third: a picture of the car's backseat, flash on, blood-red. BABY deleted the texts quickly before shuffling off to the bathroom. *Pull*, she thought. *Don't look away.*

Being undone in her bathroom was its own form of intimacy. BABY peeled off her clothes, skin meeting the floor with a sizzle. After the split occurred, lying on the tile was a kiss of cool, was a cool slipping river, was a sweet river rushing. Phone, dress, body—check. Wallet, underwear, purse—check. How ready is BABY to speak plainly? The dripping faucet kept time to the pace of her heart as the room rushed around her, opened its unfilled bathtub like a palm and made way for her. She slid in.

The word *vagina* comes from the Latin word meaning *sword-sheath*. A hole to rest a weapon in. "Maybe," BABY's therapist will muse, "you need to feel like sex is taken from you in order for it to feel morally justified." Yes—that's it: incurable fantasies of being taken and fucked culminating in one night of untamed pain in a parking lot. Later, BABY will log into her social media accounts to look at his most recent posts: photos of his child grinning big and wide on a swing at a park, others of his child's first birthday party, both of them eating cake, blue balloons twisted in the wind. BABY will indulge in her own wish-fulfillment fantasy: big wrought-iron hunks of locks so heavy on her pelvis she wouldn't be able to leave her bed even if she wanted to. God's little hole would have finally learned her lesson.

She's dreaming—and let her dream. What she has to say is not easy. Imagine your soul in its most ideal container. What container is that? A room with broken windows, the chamber left behind in a pitted cherry. The body she was three hours ago and the body she is now twist in and out of each other like two snakes slithering out of a jar.

The window is her portal to nowhere, and the black road receives her as she is. The hundreds of small knives lit in the sky bend toward her and press into her stomach, punching in and slicing upwards. Organs like jewels jumble and push through the incision. At the top of her stomach, the body she was three hours ago stretches out a hand covered in motor oil, stinking like gasoline. *I know you*, BABY thinks and grips tightly onto the hand to pull. Bile rises up in the back of her throat as the newborn thing lands on the floor with a wet thud.

Don't look away: two arms and two legs, a body with a blue dress crackling and stuck to its skin. Tangled brown hair drapes along its forehead, head, and shoulder blades. *It's another woman*, BABY realizes— unknown and unwanted, whining as it begins to rise up on all fours.

The split in BABY's body requires attention, the kind that dresses with care. The figure attempts to stand by gripping BABY's thighs and pulling up. It runs its hands along the loose flaps of skin where BABY's stomach once was and begins to seal each end of the hole together with spit. *Second skin*, it explains. *Make me make me make me*, it begs. A line of saliva glistens like a wet welcome along BABY's now woundless stomach.

The love-drunk figure leans its full weight against her, eyes closed. It's dreaming—and let it dream. BABY pushes the matted hair away from its face and sees a mirror. *My disgusting little dog, out like a light*, she thinks and laughs. She grabs the figure by both of its arms and drags it over to the bedroom. The body sliding against the carpet sounds like the ocean, like her ear pressed against a shell. In another world, she is brushing her teeth and going to bed early. She is getting ready for work. She is going on a date. BABY is eager for a lock and key as she lays its body down on the floor and runs out of the room. Only when the door is shut behind her does she feel one small moment of relief.

tv light plays with BA-BEE from the shadows at the bottom
of the door i am peaking thru   smashed to

eye level / her feet flush with the floor like two thin lips
meeting in disappointment / one more dream

to unravel me : perched   on a branch is a single blue
bird / something like love : crouched and starved

for it / i am a seed on gravel i am an angel with no
lighter wrapped in steely yellow light / in a dream

i come to BA-BEE blue bird snapped between my jaws / she
touches my   head / eases me all my right places /

one high pitched yelp from me and her feet flinch *! WHAT
DID I SAY !* and like a quick right turn / like

the feeling i got when BA-BEE locked the door / a fraction
of a second pacing over and over again the same floor

God never said it was easy, did he? He presented BABY with a door and no clear instructions on how to get through it. She checks to make sure her bedroom is locked again before collapsing onto the couch in the living room. Each surface of the house smells of sweat and blood, as if the house, too, was birthed from her tonight. *Everywhere is God's container*, she thinks. God is in the walls. God is in the leather seats of the red car. God is in the fingerprints on her thighs. Everywhere except for inside of her.

And what was inside of her? Both dog and woman in form and spirit: champion of competitive obedience, blind devotion. Has it ever known vertical life? Was it born to be laid out, dried flat? It's easier to believe that fault could be placed elsewhere. She wonders if that's what it's here for—it's the thrill of taking ownership, the body for beating and not the brains.

Every now and then, her Dog Woman groans and throws her body at the door, the sound so heavy the world nearly breaks. BABY shoots up from the couch to scream at her, *WHAT DID I SAY?* As she moves, her legs shift and the fingerprints come into the light again. *Why didn't you lick this shit off,* BABY complains and covers them. God is an intrusive thought. God is a crushed bug on her windshield begging to be wiped. BABY turns on the television, alternating the volume between normal and ear-splitting. She would've liked to have seen the exact moment Dog Woman realized she wasn't coming back for her—would've savored it, watching her two dim eyes flood with tears. BABY turns up the volume even more.

The newest show on television is about a man who becomes a time traveler in order to find his wife before she dies, but in each reality he only finds her body. It is ten episodes long, but by the second, BABY is no longer surprised, just watches to find out where the body will be next. Once in a sarcophagus, once in a boat floating on top of the water, once propped up on a chair in a kitchen, a lit cigarette smoking up the room. Time Traveler opens a window for her as if that still matters.

time traveler on television has a team
of / people who ask over the radio
when /   are you now / sometimes the
prop department has conveniently
placed a / calendar / some times he
answers *i don't* / *know* / team of people
wait / with bated breath their voice an
anchor to the present / *when are you now*
/ dog-woman is a symphony of
weeping and gnashing of teeth
bound / by time but i don't relent /
when are you now / time traveler has
someone to stay alive for / time
traveler orders a meal with protein and
nutrients and team of people sigh in
relief over the radio *tell us* / *everything*
they're wishing *did you* / *find her* / time
traveler is kept alive through a series of
dinners and knob cranking / so am i

in the dress in the dress before her an uneasy second skin

in the dress from three hours ago before her, uneasy

image of dog- woman curled in a ball licking the pit of her knee cap till it's raw

image of the orange light of one cigarette suspended

in baby's hand burning into nothing, sky

the color of shame violet and hot

to the touch

god with camera in hand and taking till your last breath

image of piss streaming down dog-woman's shivering legs

the smell like the back of a dead animal's throat

image of baby scrubbing at the inside of her thigh over the bathtub

skin,

now spotless

her thoughts turn to dog-woman who bit off

the world to be born

(if i let you out i let out your sick too)

time traveler stands in front of a locked door glances behind him

as if saying goodbye to his life before stepping through

i don't need you i don't need you i don't need you i don't need you i don't need you i don't need you i don't i don't
need you i don't need you i don't need you i don't need you i don't need you i don't need you i don't need
you i don't need you i don't *(if i—)* need you i don't need you i don't need you i don't need you i don't need
you i don't need you i don't need you i don't need you i don't need you i don't need you i don't need you i
don't need you i don't need you i don't need **so does baby : adrift at the threshold** you i don't need you i
don't need you i don't need you i don't need you i don't need you i don't need you i don't need you i don't
need you i don't need you i don't need you i don't need you i don't need you i don't need you i don't need
you i don't need you i don't *(if i did not—)* need you i don't need you i don't need you i don't need you i don't
need you i don't need you i don't need you i don't need you i don't need you i don't need you i don't need
you i don't need you i don't need you i don't need you i don't need you i don't need you i don't need you i
don't need you i don't need you i don't **the room has been quiet now for hours** need you i don't need you i
don't need you i don't need you i don't need you i don't need you i don't **key in lock and turn** need you i
don't need you i don't need you i don't need you i don't need you i don't need you i don't need you i don't
need you i don't need you i don't need you i don't need you i don't need you i don't need you i don't need
you i don't need you i don't need you i don't need *(if i did not want—)* you i don't need you i don't need you i
don't need you i don't need you i don't need you i don't need you i don't need you i don't need you i don't
need you i don't need you i don't need you i don't need you i don't need you i don't need you i don't need
you i don't need you i don't need you i don't need you i don't need **baby peeks in** don't need you i don't
need you i don't need you i don't need you i don't need you i don't need you i don't need you i don't need
you i don't need you **image of dog-woman fast asleep** i don't **dirty** need **sprawled** you i don't need you i
don't need you i don't need you i don't need you i don't need you need you i don't need you i don't need you
i don't need you i don't need you **dress like crumpled paper riding** i don't **up** need you i don't need you i
don't need you i don't need you i don't need you i don't need you i don't need you i don't need you i don't
need you i don't need you i don't need you i don't need you i don't need you i don't need you i don't need
you i don't need you i don't need you i don't need you i don't need *(if i did not want i would not—)* you i don't
need you i don't need you i don't need you i don't need you i don't need you i don't need you i don't need
you i don't need you i don't need you i don't need you i don't need you i don't need you i don't need you i
don't need you i don't need you i don't need you i don't need **there: three red fingerprints** you i don't need
you i don't need you i don't need you i don't need you i don't need you i don't need you i don't need you i
don't need you i don't need you i don't **the sight of it** need you i don't **unraveling** need you i don't need you i
don't need you i don't need you i don't need you i don't need you i don't need you i don't need you i don't
need you i don't need you i don't need you i don't need you i don't need you i don't need you i don't need

you i don't need you i don't need you i don't need you i don't need *(if i did not want i would not look)* you i don't
need you i don't need you i don't need you i don't need you i don't need you i don't need you i don't i don't
need you i don't need you i don't need you i don't need you i don't need you i don't need you i don't need
you i don't **shut the door** need you you i don't need you i don't need you i don't need you i don't need you i
don't need you i don't need **slide to the ground** you i don't need you i don't need you i don't need you i don't
need you i don't need you i don't need you i don't need you i don't need you i don't need you i don't need
you i don't need you i don't need you i don't need **the room's light cuts sharp** you **across baby's face** i don't
need you i don't need you i don't need you i don't need you i don't need you i don't need you i don't need
you i don't need you i don't need you **god's finger on the shutter** i don't need you i don't need you i don't
need you i don't need you i don't need you i don't need you i don't need you i don't need you i don't need
you i don't need you i don't need you i don't need you i don't need *(look——)* you i don't need you i don't need
you i don't need you i don't need you i don't need you i don't need you i don't need you i don't need you i
don't need you i don't need you i don't need you i don't **let it break you and** need you i don't need you **smile** i
don't need you i don't need you i don't need you i don't need you i don't need you i don't need you i don't
need you i don't need you i don't need you i don't need you i don't need you i don't need you i don't need
you i don't need you i don't need you i don't need you i don't need you i don't need you i don't need you i
don't need you i don't need you i don't need you i don't need you i don't need you i don't need you i don't
need you i don't need you i don't need you i don't need you i don't need you i don't need you i don't need
you i don't need you i don't need you i don't need you i don't need you i don't need you i don't need you i
don't need you i don't need you i don't need you i don't need you i don't need you i don't need you i don't
need you i don't need you i don't need you i don't need you i don't need you i don't need you i don't need
you i don't need you i don't need you i don't need you i don't need you i don't need you i don't need you i
don't need you i don't need you i don't need you i don't need you i don't need you i don't need you i don't
need you i don't need you i don't need you i don't need you i don't need you i don't need you i don't need
you i don't need you i don't need you i don't need you i don't need you i don't need you i don't need you i
don't need you i don't need you i don't need you i don't need you i don't need you i don't need you i don't
need you i don't need you i don't need you i don't need you i don't need you i don't need you i don't need

while dog-woman and i over- / lapped
one another in mourning / posture
that night i dreamt i was going blind /
it happened slowly—first my right eye
fizzled / the left later lost in sleep /
right / before i had orgasmed twice
and each / time a man lifted up my
drooling head to present on a platter to
an empty room / each time the man
said *you* / *like it when i tell you what to do* /
don't you / and as figures materialized
i / faded away / dog-woman and i's
first night together was filled with
fear / from the wild she tended toward
/ the fringes / we had to stabilize
ourselves any way we knew how / her
fingers slip out from underneath the
door / tempted / to lay mine to hers /
tempted to nail us both to the floor /
name an item in the room i said to her /
name every item you see until i come back for
you

panting in the dark room : my cage green

       table blue lamp white jeans yellow carpet pink

condoms red vibrator on small table only other fabric

      i've worn folded   with lightest   touch floral scent

carried on the back of a fan humming its wheezing

      song breeze   -d thru window its silver looking glass

testing the stay   filing down my teeth browning the backs

      of my eyeballs   thrusting ceiling spinning

vase nothing beside me but her bed / her mirror

The kitchen is a place of grief. In the refrigerator, BABY finds one moldy squash, four spongy apples, three-week-old lo mein in a blue-fuzzed hue. On the counter is a mortar and pestle she's never used. On the table is a cake platter meant for her head. If she stands still for long enough, she can hear a man who waits for her outside of the house, his voice slinking in through her headphones: *tell me who this pussy belongs to—* BABY makes eyes with the bottle of vodka in the freezer. *Thank God.* She grabs it.

Time is useless when it is three in the afternoon and you're drunk. Time is ideal when you spend most of it detached from your body. She recalls the shared puddle of drool between her and Dog Woman this morning—how it pooled underneath the door as if from one endless mouth, no beginning or end to either of them. That kind of connection has never been hers before. Time Traveler would walk into BABY's house and unlock the bedroom door. Time Traveler was born to show mercy, to look for his beloved in the cupboards, under the couch.

However long Dog Woman had been in there, it was long enough. BABY moves toward the door, trembling, and inserts the key into the lock. Dog Woman whines through her teeth when she hears the click and pushes through as soon as the door opens, only to fumble toward the coffee table in the living room, crawl belly to the ground to hide underneath it.

The house lets out one big breath. Small bits of broken glass crunch under BABY's feet as she approaches Dog Woman. *What are you doing here?* BABY asks and unscrews the bottle to drink. *What do you want from me?* Dog Woman doesn't take the bait, trying to be still as the table she's under shakes with her nerves. *I thought about killing you,* BABY says, *because that would be killing me.* And this time, with an understanding of the chain between them, BABY relents: *Little wife from my rib, why must I keep you?*

Dog Woman doesn't understand what BABY means through the fog of her immediate needs: the dryness of her mouth, the filth all over her skin, the itch between her shoulder blades. She contorts her body as much as possible but can't quite reach. Dog Woman avoids BABY's eyes and cries into nothing. From one trap to another: BABY is suddenly sorry she has failed to be more hopeful or more kind.

Hey, she tries again. *What's supposed to happen after this?* She gestures around the house and bends down so that she's level with Dog Woman, who finally looks from BABY's bottle to her eyes and back again as her fingertips graze the edge of BABY's arm.

Is that water? Dog Woman asks. *Do you love me?*

i am what they call a   romantic   or at least my BA-BEE says so / once i sensed

a wet gray cloud over BA-BEE and with flowers in my teeth i came to her—she asked *when*

are you now and i didn't want to say any   where else but here with you so i dropped

the bundle and / open-mouthed / waited for the moment to pass / drool

dripping / twirling covering the stems in clear ooze now looking softer / more   blue / made

more enjoyable for her by my body or at least i hoped so / in the woods outside

this house i am another sort of creature : lingered upon / his eye undressing me / in all

of my nakedness i dream of her   of being carried deep in our body / marred in marrow

resplendent in glistening stomach / *it is not realistic to be so tender* BA-BEE said /

OF ALL the things she should know about me first she should know i'll love her

in any way i'm allowed

image of baby and dog-woman in imperfect pietá :

dog-woman's long and sticky

torso at baby's feet

baby's hand scrunched in her hair

a first touch can happen like this :

indifferent but still binding

the hole in the woods calls out to dog-woman—

a brand new need boiling in her cauldron

the hole has a name :

headphones-man

who each night licks his chops

orders more of her to go

anything can look like dinner if you just squint

hard enough he says

while eating you i eat her too

each night dog-woman adopts the position and pushes backwards

into the past—skin so meat malleted

her body is an island she is stranded on

there is no god in losing he says

and i am making you lose

he doesn't know how wrong he is :

god is in the blood between them

god is in the slow crawl back to the house

god is the look in baby's eye like a stone wrapped

around her ankle like

regret, the shadow of love

if anything

dog-woman is her historian

she is here to show her what he's done

on the menu tonight: nightmare fuel
our soup du jour sipped for dinner /
dog-woman / limps home to her bed /
news- / papers feathered like soft
pillows / *i like it like this* she says /
whimpers / at the border of it /
evening draws a shade over us / is the
glass of water i reach for in the dark /
body isn't yours body is someone else's she
chews dreamily on a bone /
preoccupied / with another oral
fixation / pill bottles lined end to end
on the kitchen table in a slow parade /
two of my cigarettes ground into her
bed / to find the begging built in is just
to find the instruction manual

quitting : every cigarette a tiny torpedo
i shoot down the lungs / dog-woman
at my feet / jaw full of wiggling
creature / whining her high-pitched
eager all over my shoes / i husband her
into a hole until she goes off to sulk in
a corner / quick to try and make me
feel / wrong as she muddies my
comforter into a giant bruise i have to
sleep / under every night / psychiatrist
prescribes xanax for grocery
shopping / we both know i'll eat
whatever comes out of dog-woman's
mouth anyway / my provider
extraordinaire : i scoop the tiny bloody
thing onto my cutting board each night
/ rat & vegetable stew / squirrel
spaghetti bolognese / trinkets of her
love

dog-woman makes trust look easy /
un- / thinking / overthinking / a ripe
pomegranate sits on the kitchen table
soaking in the light waiting / to be split
/ dog-woman watches me pluck and
tweeze and scrub from the bathroom
doorway / how long till i understand
her if / ever / slow to language she
nuzzles my calf / slow to touch i slip /
down / her cheek in my hand my
brush gliding through / her hair
snagging on / tiny islands of dirt and
rock / there is a god who closes
wombs like drawing curtains / that
kind of power looks good when our
cunt does nothing but bleed / i draw
the bath / soak our body in the
warmed water / hand over fingerprints
/ for better or worse / forever or just
this once i owe you

first time i met BA-BEE she had no idea what to do with me / i trembled in and looked into

her / eye to eye / neither of us knew what form i would take on but on hands and knees we

recognized each other / days later she let me follow her into the kitchen where she

slipped an oily meat disc out of a bag and called it *bologna* / strange to discover that the hole

in the middle of me was also for pleasure / and at the sight of my lips stretching / teeth

mushing she let go the most beautiful sound : a trill like someone had run their fingers over

strings as they passed by and i /

fell in love with that sound / i didn't know

the term for falling in love at first / BA-BEE watches television in which those who look

like BA-BEE but are not BA-BEE talk and hand each other flowers / gripped

up from the wild in order to communicate tenderness / BA-BEE read to me from the

dictionary on good nights and once spilled the meaning of it : showing gentleness /

sensitivity to pain / easy to chew / other uses : *to tenderize* where in BA-BEE grabbed a meat mallet to execute the concept on a raw animal breast / with each

strike the breast was left with spiked imprints / broken tissue

next she agreed to let me

see the world / loaded me up into a car and shut the lid on me / this was unlike

the other car i've seen : at each stop the door remain unlocked / BA-BEE made

me sit straight in the front seat / made me keep my head in while we drove / movement

with no exhaustion / entire lives passed us by : other / containers more woods

and the long paved pathways that got us here SO MUCH to take in it whipped

my brain into days past :: before my heart broke

out of my chest / licking sea breeze

car exhaust smoked air body odor salty on my / tongue / a thermometer to the world /

BA-BEE said *! NOT SO LOUDLY !* / i had not realized i was yowling :

the kind of noise you pour into an empty universe just to fill it / the outside leaked

in highlighting the side of her face beaming and yes the thing called love leapt

into my chest / a love which i had never tasted before

in the tenth episode time traveler opened one final door : **in this room there was no body** **only a desk and a potter's wheel and god** **in his studio of wax** **alongside thousands of angels** **armed with lighters** **flicking the hourglass** **teasing the end** **team of angels asked** *(when are you now)* **as the woods spun on the potter's wheel to reveal one torn blue dress** *(when are you now)* **every body begins with a dream** : **a lump of clay** **a dress in two** **a woman and her half split across two seats** **one looks when the other is not looking** **one tucks her hair behind her ear and rests her head** **on the open window strands spilling** **into the wind like streamers** **all of earth felt the sting of heat that day** as the flames grew hotter and hotter

as the wheel spun faster   exhausted   grinding up against the wound

and god, trapped by time, could not fix it

in this world we are treated to god's catalogue of regret—

what he has coveted with his gaze :

every hair on their head, numbered

every scar on their body, its shape and color, memorized

god was born to show mercy

god was born to look for the dog and her woman in the earth's green pit

in the orange-tinged bathtub   in the room bubbling with wax

time traveler saw the jagged tree in the distance

he could feel the end coming from miles away and still ran toward it

image of dog and woman in the car as it glides sweet

the song that plays on the radio,

their favorite—god documents

i love you i love you i love you i love you i love you i love you i **as a smile stretches across two faces**
you i love you i love you i love you i love you i love you i love you i love you i love you i love you i love
you i love you i love you i love you i love you i love you i love you i love you i love you i love you i love
you i love you i love you i love you i love you i love you i love you i love you i love you i love you i love
you i love you i love you i love you i love you i love you i love you i love you i love you i love you i love
you i love you i love you i love you i love you i love you i love you i love you i love you i love you i love
you i love you i love you i love you i love you i love you i love you i love you i love you i love you i love
you i love you i love you i love you i love you i love you i love you i love you i love you i love you i love
you i love you i love you i love you i love you i love you i love you i love you i love you i love you i love
you i love you i love you i love you i love you i love you i love you i love you i love you i love you i love
you i love you i love you i love you i love you i love you i love you i love you i love you i love you i love
you i love you i love you i love you i love you i love you i love you i love you i love you i love you i love
you i love you i love you i love you i love you i love you i love you i love you i love you i love you i love
you i love you i love you i love you i love you i love you i love you i love you i love you i love you i love
you i love you i love you i love you i love you i love you i love you i love you i love you i love you i love
you i love you i love you i love you i love you i love you i love you i love you i love you i love you i love
you i love you i love you i love you i love you i love you i love you i love you i love you i love you i love
you i love you i love you i love you i love you i love you i love you i love you i love you i love you i love
you i love you i love you i love you i love you i love you i love you i love you i love you i love you i love
you i love you i love you i love you i love you i love you i love you i love you i love you i love you i love
you i love you i love you i love you i love you i love you i love you i love you i love you i love you i love
you i love you i love you i love you i love you i love you i love you i love you i love you i love you i love
you i love you i love you i love you i love you i love you i love you i love you i love you i love you i love
you i love you i love you i love you i love you i love you i love you i love you i love you i love you i love
you i love you i love you i love you i love you i love you i love you i love you i love you i love you i love
you i love you i love you i love you i love you i love you i love you i love you i love you i love you i love
you i love you i love you i love you i love you i love you i love you i love you i love you i love you i love
you i love you i love you i love you i love you i love you i love you i love you i love you i love you i love
you i love you i love you i love you i love you i love you i love you i love you i love you i love you i love

A knock, a dull droning beat pulls Dog Woman and BABY out of their sleep. Dog Woman's ears perk up. Her body, ritualed to death, rises up off of the bed. She can feel where her attention is demanded.

Snacks for the road? BABY jokes with nowhere for it to land. More hopeful, she summons, more kind. *Sorry,* she says.

Dog Woman sheds her clothes on her way to the woods: dress, underwear, socks—check. *If I don't go who else will,* she says, dropping the truth between them. The look in her eye pours out until she's naked, tail-bone tucked and damp and gone.

Dog Woman's last look is illegible. It contains multitudes. BABY the executioner turns her eyes to the ground as she passes through the door without a sound. Time knows exactly what it wants, and it is ruthless.

i know many stories but none as well as headphones-man : he / pauses   reaches to turn

up the knob at the front of the car / the air is so cool the tips of my fingers frost

to the window / him and me in the middle of the woods / again / he asks me *are you a GOOD*

girl and how does a GOOD girl behave / dick is drill is the end of my life as he slides

the transformation in dry / what he really wants to know is how tight my BAD is: speculumed

wide open breezy all inside breezy heart spun   right out

                                                 he says he says so much and fills my

brainwaves / did you know once i was a dream in a room and now i'm a body yanked / back

to a blasting radio / a song like a victory lashes out at me and headphones-man begins to dance /

he lifts my head / finds it limp / *come on* he says *sing* / my mouth is a well i've fallen into / *you're*

no fun he says and says so much it's hard to keep track only remember GOOD and GIRL

i am / neither but was born to keep the fantasy alive little good little girl little blood trickling

little stream lapping up the leftover me-juice

vomiting in the toilet :
executioner's day
off / so drunk my
home broke
in half / still
a vision
drops by :
headphones-man
puts a hand
through my chest /
i can finally see
his face / all this
time
shrouded in
darkness—his
brow screwed
in a perpetual
pig-grunt / he
shouts
i'm coming he

///

rips / my spectral
predator / he wants

me
to feel it doesn't
he / swimming out
of after-birth
haze to what could
be who / dog-
woman / my
second
chance : i open
my eyes to still water
in a porcelain
bowl of
shit / the bathroom
stained
brown / metal
faucets
hiss with
rust / my body's
odor as sharp
as the desire
for the end of my
life / it all creeps
up my nose into
my brain where
i register the one
quiet thing radiating

warmth in my
kitchen : surrounded
by milk ejaculate
and congealed
filth is one / blue
bird laid out
on my cutting
board / a blue
descendant of
the sky / this bird
whose throat was
carefully slit

//

drained /
three feathers
fanned on each
end / a love
letter or a good-
bye / how long
ago did she
leave me / time
slipped
out of
reach / along the
backyard a thin red

trail is still
warm /
does she want
me to follow
her / only
one way to find out :
i crawl
off into the woods /
nose pressed
against her
blood road

//

has it always been
like this / i had friends i
went to parties / woke
up every day
and brushed my teeth /
my / hair / clocked
in and clocked
out / with each
push forward my
memory
fumbles over
twigs greased with
rainwater over mulched

leaves crawling
with night worms all
pressing
against my bare
legs / headphones-
man murdered
us in every life-

//

time / dog-
woman can i
recall our most
recent night
together :
you / freshly clean /
having rolled around
in the backyard all
morning feeling
earth-bound
and spreading it
all over my
sofa / you freshly
clean / kneel
in your corner of
the bedroom /
did you know

and—of course
you knew—of ruth
who was told to
uncover
her master's feet
and lie
at the edge of his
bed / crossing
the threshold to wed
him—/ were you
thinking of her
when i approached /
my hand threaded
into the roots
of your hair / lifting
your eyes
upward
to me / i could feel
headphones-man
inside of
me then : my
brain-melter / *who
owns you ?* i asked
/ and your
eyes pooled with
tears / if i tug
your head the hairs

on the back of my
neck are pulled
too / some-
times the most we
can do is
show no
resistance / try
to be a well-
oiled face fuck even
when
that's not all we are

///

imagine the strain
that can put on
a connection / blame
it on my gemini
rising my / venus
in aries / born to
be demanding
and indifferent and
craving / horoscope
the next morning
read : *focus on
the suffering of those
around you / you're*

hot and everyone
knows it / a sharp
rock slices my
leg to bring
me back to
the present / the
woods
somehow darker
than a few hours
ago and colder / i
lie on my back /
cradle
my knee to my
chest / the sky above
me splits open to
reveal a black
slab of nothing-
ness / am i
hot does / everyone
know it

the bucket i have become is unbearable / memory gargling can
make a bitch   tired / will make the throat weary /

                                        forest
looking more and more like it needs to be razed the thicker it
goes / all too painful to remember headphones-man full of
anger at the blood i left on the back-

                           seat of his car / *all over* he
said *all consuming* and *i scrubbed all night* / i wish i had watched
him / erotica á la violence / i push through thorns mossy rocks
into a clearing / i have never come this far before / the air is
sweeter here packed with sweat

                             and humidity / the
greenery bursts from the earth as the land plunges into a deep
valley / it's the sound that marks my arrival : the slap of a body
penetrating another / once again dog-woman arches for my
forgiveness in the middle of our brain /

                                aching for pills or
food or alcohol / yearning for my bed, my home with four
walls and locks / it's impossible to avert my eyes from my own
unbecoming /

                        dog-woman do you remember how the dust
and dirt caked on you each night you came home / the
unchecked hair all over your body acting as a net for remnants
of headphones-man, his appetite dried in your crevices / i
lowered you into our bathtub, brimming with

soapy water /

    you winced as it licked each cut, whining out the
tension held in your legs and shoulders / we had a language you
and i : the ebb and flow of our breath into one another as we
locked the door on the world and shut off the lights / it was
hard to be seen after such a

          rupture / your chin
resting in my one hand, a cup in my other, i began to cleanse
you / the bathtub

     reddened around your body one waterfall at a
time / your trust slipping in and out of me buttered by our
touch / *baay-beee* at your lips in a long unwieldy cry / *make me*
you began but never finished before breaking

          out my name
again / *make me make me make me* / fullness was the thing we
were after / headphones-man's voice cuts the air: *are you*

        are you a good girl /
the word *good* has roots in seizing, gathering / when he asks us
if we are good, he is looking to bind us / at the bottom of the
valley there's a rusted red car, leftover metal the earth has
started to swallow with tentacles of ivy and moss / dog-woman
must have to crawl

     through the back window to get in / the way
is steep / with no obvious path no *yes* or *no* marked clear i begin
going down

my BA-BEE wore nothing when she came to see me / my BA-BEE pickled with dirt and

skin / my BA-BEE no more wholesome than the first day i met her / upside down / pinned

here for some time / loose and slurring / aura hazing / but at the sight of her

an untouchable thing like a spirit or a dream trampled through me / glancing up through

my lashes / to take another look at her / descending / the car has a new smell today like burnt

butter / like an oil-slick biscuit / like a tornado in a juice glass / as his sweat drips

down on me i swat it like a fly and continue to watch / keeping watch over someone

requires all four corners of my attention / it is the same as when BA-BEE thought i could

learn tricks / offered me food / asked me to / *WAIT* she warned / and her *JUST*

left a delicious little snail trail until — / *GO* /

i never understood these moments until i

learned about devotion / something i saw as BA-BEE flipped through pictures of him

on her computer every day like i couldn't / notice / her eyes fishbowls of love and sorry / my BA-BEE is the leaves at the wrong end of a tea cup / the needle

at the bottom of a ball pit / i asked her what devotion was and she asked me where i'd heard

a word like that / not caring about my answer she powered down her computer

and explained it is to take / a hammer to something to set it apart / to call it

yours /

my BA-BEE wore my heart across her forehead like a new bandana as she neared

the rear window / my BA-BEE rolled the dice and lost and came for me

anyway / my BA-BEE on her white horse buckling into me full speed / sometimes

headphones-man cums and sometimes he doesn't / or maybe he does every time

and i've stopped noticing / *look at me* he says / off-script / even when i want

to look at him i can't do it / this must have been how it happened to you

BA-BEE / you know i bite the bit and let you steer me / you know the biggest love

letter i write to you is my body being able to take it /

                                                            BA-BEE is coming up

behind him / all of headphones-man is focused on having me he knows nothing else / in her eyes a sprinkle of that devotion or pain in the midst of the wet

our gushing wound has created / no moon

here in the middle of the woods :

BA-BEE's teeth glitter under the light of a single bulb hung from the sky / spinning

in the wind her anger grinds against her like a red baseball bat to the face blooming

into full vision as she tethers our millions of lives to the backseat of the car

and drags herself onto it / with no other option she opens her mouth wide and bites

down / teeth sinking into headphones-man's neck with a sloppy crunch / his jaw

goes slack / his eyes grow black / my BA-BEE flips the switch and unlocks

the door / my BA-BEE pulls his drill out of me and sloughs off his body

like an old suit jacket

/ fever dreams now wrung dry / his body as solid as mine /

as slick / will i ever love another woman who would kill for me ? / BA-BEE

says *i bought you some clothes i* / *will bring you home for a bath* / it can't be it can't

be / sky and blue bird a single color the end of us the final hallway we split through

to reconvene though not yet / i begin to roll up into myself and last i see her begging *stay with me* / and last i hear her drumming out against the leather seat

of the car our own special incantation : *make me make me make me* or she hears me

or i hear her / all our voices blending into choral agony a mess so beautiful

they'll tell stories as they mop us up for days

Acknowledgments

"A ROMANTIC" and "SMASHED TO" have been previously published under different titles in the *Driftwood 2024 Anthology* and the *Driftwood 2025 Anthology* with Driftwood Press. Prior versions of select poems are published online with Metatron Press as a part of an author feature for The Metatron Prize for Rising Authors 2021 shortlist.

Thank you to Kristiane, Eliza, and the Harbor Editions team who have been so kind and gracious in helping me make *Dog Woman* a reality.

This chapbook would be nothing without Paula Rego's truly astounding body of work. The love she poured into the *Dog Woman* series reached out across the world and into me and I finally felt free.

Thank you to my beautiful friends for their endless love and support (Hadassah, Liam, David, Brandon, Colleen--love you forever!). Thank you to Jill for understanding the vision so perfectly with their incredible artwork. Thank you to Evangeline who saw the good and desperate thing in *Dog Woman* early on and believed in her with a devotion that sometimes rivaled my own.

Loving repeating is the best way of being (as Gertrude says) and there'd be no poems without loving repeating these songs:

1. "High Horse" - Mannequin Pussy
2. "Cop Car" - Mitski
3. "Pain" - Boy Harsher
4. "Gimme All Your Love" - Alabama Shakes
5. "Relay" - Fiona Apple

And, finally, to my beloved Dog Woman: I like to think of time as simultaneous. I like to think back to that moment many years ago and know that as we were in the car, we were also already outside of it—both of us crawling out with one muddied hand in front of the other, living a great big life, laughing our way into the future.

Melinda Freudenberger is a poet living in Brooklyn, NY with their cat, Amy. They graduated from The New School in 2020 with their MFA in Poetry. *Dog Woman* is their debut chapbook. Find more of their work at melindafreudenberger.com.

About Small Harbor Publishing

Small Harbor Publishing is a 501c3 nonprofit organization. Our goal is to publish unique and diverse voices. We are a feminist press, and we are committed to diversity and inclusion. We strive to bring new voices to a devoted and expanding readership.

Small Harbor Publishing began in 2018 with the first issue of *Harbor Review*. The magazine is an online space where poetry and art converse. *Harbor Review* quickly grew and now publishes reviews and runs multiple micro chapbook competitions, including the Washburn Prize and the Editor's Prize.

In July 2020, Small Harbor Publishing was officially incorporated and began Harbor Editions. Harbor Editions accepts submissions through a chapbook open reading period, a hybrid chapbook open reading period, the Marginalia Series, and the Laureate Prize.

In 2023, Harbor Anthologies began with a mission to promote texts that explore social justice issues and highlight marginalized writers.

If you would like to support Small Harbor Publishing, visit our "About" page at: smallharborpublishing.com/about.